THE GREAT
WESTERN RAILWAY

Tim Bryan

SHIRE PUBLICATIONS

Published by Shire Publications Ltd.
PO Box 883, Oxford, OX1 9PL, UK
PO Box 3985, New York, NY 10185-3985, USA
Email: shire@shirebooks.co.uk   www.shirebooks.co.uk

First published 2010.
Transferred to digital print on demand 2016.

A CIP catalogue record for this book is available from the
British Library.

Shire Library no. 595   ·   ISBN-13: 978 0 74780 788 9

Tim Bryan has asserted his right under the Copyright,
Designs and Patents Act, 1988, to be identified as the
author of this book.

Designed by Tony Truscott Designs, Sussex, UK.
Typeset in Perpetua and Gill Sans.
Printed and bound by PrintOnDemand-Worldwide.com,
Peterborough, UK

Cover image

A GWR 'King' class locomotive on a West of England
express speeds along the sea front at Dawlish. The image
is a detail from a 1935 Great Western Railway Centenary
poster.

Title page image

A poster celebrating and advertising Great Western
express services between Paddington and Birmingham
Snow Hill. Although the new two-hour route was
inaugurated just before the First World War, this poster
dates from the 1920s.

Contents page image

One of Churchward's 'Saint' Class two-cylinder 4-6-0s at
the head of an express near Twyford. The rolling stock is
painted in the crimson lake that was used during the
Edwardian period.

Acknowledgements

Thanks are due to: Elaine Arthurs, Collections Officer at
STEAM Museum of the Great Western Railway, Swindon;
Roger Trayhurn, Swindon Library; Laurence Waters, Great
Western Trust Didcot; and the photographic team at the
British Motor Industry Heritage Trust.

I am grateful to the individuals and institutions who have
allowed me to reproduce illustrations for the book, which
are acknowledged as follows:

Unless otherwise credited, photographs are from the
collection of STEAM: Museum of the Great Western
Railway Swindon, with the following exceptions:
Great Western Trust, pages 28 (top), 29 (top), 41 (top),
and 43 (bottom); Swindon Libraries, pages 14, 15, and 21
(bottom); private collection, pages 4, 24, and 25; Bill
Wright, page 54; author's own collection, 22, 36, 46 (top
and middle), 50, 58 (bottom), 60 (top & bottom), and 61.

Shire Publications is supporting the Woodland Trust, the UK's leading woodland conservation charity, by funding the dedication of trees.

CONTENTS

INTRODUCTION

The GWR's trademark lined Brunswick Green livery never looked better than when set off by Indian Red frames (black was used after 1906). This is one of Churchward's famous 'Saint' class – one of a number built as 4-4-2s to test the efficacy of this then-popular wheel arrangement.

Throughout its history the Great Western Railway (GWR) was characterised by a confidence and swagger that could be seen as bordering on arrogance. From the time of Brunel, the GWR had always gone its own way, beginning with the bold but doomed experiment of building a line in what became known as the 'broad' gauge, with its rails 7 feet, ¼-inch apart, rather than the 'standard' gauge, the 4 feet 8½ inches used by the Stephensons and dismissively called 'coal wagon' gauge by GWR staff. The Great Western continued in this vein, often out of step with other lines in both design and operating practices.

The broad gauge was abolished in 1892, but by then Brunel's original line from Bristol to London had been extended to cover much of the West Country, Wales and the west Midlands. Within two decades the GWR was the most forward-looking railway of the time, investing millions of pounds in new lines, locomotives, rolling stock and stations.

After the First World War the Great Western had not only to recover from the conflict itself but also to cope with the upheaval caused by the 'Grouping' of railways into the 'Big Four'. This trauma was followed by industrial unrest that culminated in the General Strike of 1926, the collapse of its coal business and the Wall Street Crash.

The inter-war era is seen by many as a high point for the GWR. Holidaymakers were whisked to the West Country on luxurious expresses such as the 'Cornish Riviera Limited', hauled by powerful locomotives of the 'King' and 'Castle' classes, built at the company's workshops at Swindon, where more than twelve thousand men constructed the engines, carriages and wagons that made the GWR so famous. Away from the holiday resorts, thousands of more humble passenger and goods trains ran on a network that by 1939 employed more than seventy thousand staff.

The Great Western played a crucial part in the Second World War, evacuating thousands of children to the countryside and, although under attack from enemy bombing, running thousands of troop and munitions trains before and after D-Day. It had hardly recovered from the conflict when it was nationalised in 1948. The independence it had shown before nationalisation continued into the British Railways era, and much of the railway survives today, despite the attention of the 'Beeching Axe'.

Above all, the GWR is remembered by many for what would now be called its corporate image. Its engines were turned out of Swindon Works in the famous 'Brunswick' green livery, with many also fitted with its trademark copper-capped chimneys and brass safety-valve covers. GWR carriages also carried the distinctive 'chocolate and cream' paint scheme for much of the company's history. The Great Western's image was also promoted through the evocative and colourful posters and publicity material produced to advertise its train services to resorts in Cornwall, Devon and other holiday destinations around its network. Long after the end of the GWR as an independent company, its pioneering spirit lives on well away from the modern railway, with a thriving network of heritage lines and museums recreating 'God's Wonderful Railway' for thousands of tourists and railway enthusiasts.

Tickets from two early constituent companies of the GWR feature in this picture as well as GWR and BR examples. As the Liskeard & Looe ticket illustrates, even dogs needed tickets to travel by rail.

BRUNEL AND THE BROAD GAUGE

ISAMBARD KINGDOM BRUNEL called the Great Western Railway 'the finest work in England'. The exploits of the flamboyant engineer dominated the early history of the company and created a network that stretched much further than the 118-mile Bristol to London route. It also included railways Brunel engineered after the completion of that line in 1841, such as the Bristol & Exeter, South Devon and Cornwall and West Cornwall railways, as well as the South Wales Railway, the Oxford, Worcester & Wolverhampton Railway and many other branches and lesser lines radiating from the main routes.

The success of early railways such as the Stockton & Darlington and the Liverpool & Manchester played a key part in persuading the business community in Bristol that a railway linking their city with the capital was essential to maintain its importance as a national centre of trade and commerce. Although there had been earlier schemes, it was not until 1833 that a meeting to 'discuss the expediency of promoting the formation of a railroad from Bristol to London' was held. With the support of such bodies as the Chamber of Commerce and the Society of Merchant Venturers, it was decided that the first step should be a survey of a route for the new line, with the cheapest tender winning the job. In a characteristic flourish, Brunel wrote to the directors, telling them that they were 'holding out a premium to the man who makes you the most flattering promises' and that he would survey a route that was the best but not necessarily the cheapest. This was undoubtedly a high-risk strategy but the gamble worked, and he was appointed engineer of the GWR in March 1833.

The directors of the new company were making a brave decision in choosing such a young (Brunel was twenty-seven) and relatively inexperienced engineer for this ambitious project. He had arrived in Bristol five years earlier to convalesce after a near-fatal accident in the Thames Tunnel, where he had been working for his father, Marc, but during his time in the city he had already gained a reputation, winning a competition to design a bridge over the Avon Gorge at Clifton and acting as consultant to the Bristol Dock Company.

Opposite:
A lithographic image of Isambard Kingdom Brunel, based on a portrait painted by his brother-in-law, John Horsley, in the 1840s. Born in 1806, the flamboyant engineer died at the age of fifty-three in 1859.

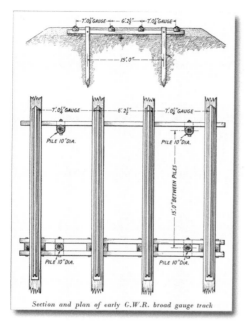

Section and plan of early G.W.R. broad gauge track

Brunel's 'baulk road', as well as being built to the broad gauge, also utilised longitudinal timbers supporting the rails, which were an inverted 'U' shape, known by the GWR as 'bridge' rail.

The GWR coat of arms, which featured the arms of the two cities it linked when it first opened in 1841: London (left) and Bristol (right).

Once appointed, Brunel undertook a full survey of the countryside over which the new railway was to run, riding the whole length of the route. A prospectus was then issued and the time-consuming and frustrating task of getting the Great Western Railway Bill through Parliament began. It took two attempts for the Act to pass, but it at last received the Royal Assent on 31 August 1835 and work began soon afterwards.

The delay in the passing of the bill had given Brunel plenty of time to plan his new line. It soon became clear that the GWR was to be unlike any other railway in existence or then being built. It would feature many innovations; the most radical was that his line would have an entirely new track gauge – 7 feet ¼ inch, known as the 'broad' gauge. Furthermore, the track formation would also be different, with rails supported longitudinally on timbers rather than using conventional sleepered track; the 'baulk road', as it became known, was characteristic of all Brunel's railway schemes, but it was the broad gauge that would eventually become a liability rather than an asset to the GWR.

The construction of the line was divided into many separate contracts for stretches of line or structures such as bridges or stations. It was estimated that the railway would cost £2,500,000 and as engineer Brunel spent long hours supervising all aspects of the project, producing drawings and specifications, meeting landowners and contractors, and riding up and down the line checking the work.

The construction of the company's London terminus was delayed since the original hope had been that the GWR would share a station with one of its rivals, the London & Birmingham (L&B), at Euston, but the arrangement was abandoned when the L&B discovered that the Great Western would be using the broad gauge. The resulting delay and lack of funds led to a temporary wooden structure serving

as the London terminus of the GWR until the early 1850s, when money was finally available to allow Brunel to build a station on a scale befitting its position as the Great Western's London base. The design of the new Paddington station owed much to the work of Joseph Paxton, the designer of the Crystal Palace. Heavily involved with many other projects, Brunel enlisted Matthew Digby Wyatt, another engineer occupied with the Great Exhibition, and asked him to provide decoration for the roof and large glazed screens at each end of the train shed.

The contractors working at either end of the line faced very different challenges. The railway crossed the Thames a number of times as it ran west from the capital. So that the railway could cross the river at Maidenhead without blocking the towpath or restricting barge traffic on the Thames, Brunel designed a bridge featuring two graceful 128-foot semi-elliptical brick arches, reputedly the flattest ever built. The first completed section of the railway opened between Paddington and Maidenhead Riverside (now Taplow) in June 1838.

A little further west, the railway was forced through a 2-mile cutting at Sonning. It was originally intended that the line should run in a much shorter tunnel there, but the excavation of the cutting turned out to be a huge battle

The original station at Paddington, seen not long after it opened in 1838. The temporary terminus had only four platforms and a very plain timber roof supported by cast-iron columns.

Maidenhead Bridge, seen in 1893 after it had been widened when the line was quadrupled. The two 128-foot spans were the flattest brick arches ever built, and Brunel's critics were convinced that it would fall down.

against the elements, with over a thousand navvies and two hundred horses struggling to move thousands of tons of spoil in dreadful winter conditions. After the failure of one of the contractors and a strike by the workmen, Brunel took control of the project and by March 1840 trains were running through to Reading from Paddington.

It was no wonder that Brunel complained about the quality of the coffee served at Swindon station. The 'infernal brew' was served from this beautiful silver model of a 'Firefly' class locomotive situated on the counter of the refreshment rooms in the 1840s.

By December 1840 the line had been completed as far as Swindon, a small market town that would be transformed by the arrival of the Great Western. Even as construction of the main line was under way, plans had also been made to build another new line, the Cheltenham & Great Western Union Railway, running north from a junction at Swindon to Gloucester and Cheltenham. The GWR was forced into an unwise but expedient lease with the contractor J. & C. Rigby, who agreed to build the station at Swindon in return for revenue from refreshment rooms to be situated there. One clause of this agreement was that all trains would stop at Swindon for ten minutes, to allow passengers to take refreshment. This arrangement led to all manner of abuses, which probably inspired the long-standing jokes about railway catering. The reputation of the place led to it being named 'Swindleum' by angry travellers.

Swindon was also chosen as the site of the Great Western's locomotive workshops by Brunel and his Locomotive Superintendent, Daniel Gooch, appointed in 1837. Twenty locomotives had originally been ordered by Brunel to his own specification from various manufacturers, but these were a mixed bag, and Gooch was obliged to spend long hours in the engine house at Paddington to keep those that did work operational. To alleviate this situation, which was exacerbated by the rapid growth of the railway, directors authorised the construction of a new 'engine establishment' at Swindon in 1841, the new facility opening in January 1843.

In contrast to the gentle gradients east of Swindon, the country to the west was characterised by steep hills and the extensive embankments and cuttings that they necessitated. Beyond Chippenham, Brunel faced his

A very early photograph of New Swindon, taken in the early 1850s. The spire of St Mark's, the railway church, is clearly visible, along with the new railway works and the cottages built for GWR employees and their families. In the foreground is the Wilts & Berks Canal.

A youthful Daniel Gooch, first Locomotive Superintendent of the GWR, photographed with a model of one of his 'Firefly' class engines. The model is now displayed at the National Railway Museum in York.

greatest challenge. After passing through a deep cutting almost 3 miles in length, trains plunge into Box Tunnel, Brunel's most impressive achievement. Driven through almost 2 miles of limestone, the tunnel was not only the product of Brunel's engineering talent but also the result of the efforts of the thousand or so navvies who laboured there for four years. Even before work began, there had been debate about the feasibility of driving a tunnel through Box Hill but, despite more problems with contractors that left Brunel and Gooch supervising the final months of the project, it finally opened on 30 June 1841, enabling trains at last to run through from Paddington to Bristol.

Brunel built Temple Meads station at Bristol in the Elizabethan style. It consisted of a castellated frontage containing offices and a boardroom, with the actual train shed built on a viaduct at first-floor level. The spacious interior, which had a 72-foot-wide mock hammerbeam roof, was built in the style of Westminster Hall in London.

Grand though these facilities were, within a few years the station had proved to be too small, particularly with the opening of lines to the West Country. A new but less grand station was built to serve trains on the Bristol

The western portal of Box Tunnel in Wiltshire, shown in a lithograph by J. C. Bourne. A railway policeman is signalling the train onwards, standing next to a Great Western 'disc and crossbar' signal.

& Exeter Railway, which was fully opened in 1844. By 1865 both had been replaced by a far larger station designed by Digby Wyatt, which catered for GWR, Bristol & Exeter and Midland Railway traffic.

The completion of the Great Western Railway from London to Bristol was marked with very little ceremony, the novelty of railways having worn off in Bristol. The project had taken its toll on Brunel's health and he realised that he could not work at the same pace as he had been doing. On subsequent projects he gave far more responsibility to a series of long-suffering assistants. Brunel concentrated on extending his broad-gauge empire into the West Country, engineering the Bristol & Exeter, South Devon, Cornwall and West Cornwall railways.

In a bid to tackle the ferociously steep gradients on the South Devon Railway (SDR) from Exeter to Plymouth, particularly on the section west of Newton Abbot, in 1844 he proposed the 'atmospheric system', a relatively new and untried idea that did not employ steam locomotives. Instead, the carriages were attached to pistons fitted inside cast-iron pipes that ran in between the rails. Air was pumped out of the pipe in front of the train, allowing atmospheric pressure behind the piston to propel the train along. This cumbersome system never worked well, and by 1848 the SDR was forced to abandon it, losing over £400,000 in the process. Brunel's reputation was badly damaged by the 'Atmospheric Caper', described by George Stephenson as a 'Great Humbug'.

The scene at Bristol in 1870. To the right is Brunel's original GWR terminus, while the Bristol & Exeter station is seen on the left. Its wooden construction is a contrast to its Great Western counterpart. A horse-drawn carriage sits on a wagon, ready to be coupled to the back of a passenger train.

Built for the GWR by Naysmyth, Gaskell & Company in 1841, 'Firefly' Class locomotive *Actaeon* was named after a hero from Greek mythology. The engine was finally withdrawn in 1868.

Further west, the engineer also created another unwelcome legacy for the company. The Cornwall and West Cornwall railways were built to very tight budgets and, to save money, Brunel designed timber viaducts to cross many of the deep river valleys along the route. On the 60 miles of the Cornwall Railway there were no fewer than forty-two of these viaducts, which, although elegant, needed careful maintenance. As trains grew heavier, they became an expensive liability and had to be replaced with brick or stone structures. The last wooden viaduct was removed in 1934.

The Cornwall Railway crossed the River Tamar from Devon to Cornwall by means of the Royal Albert Bridge at Saltash. Two enormous wrought-iron trusses, each weighing over 1,000 tons, were built at the side of the river and floated on pontoons to the centre of the channel, where they were inched 100 feet up the bridge piers into position; the first such operation was witnessed by over 300,000 people. The resulting structure, a combination of wrought-iron tubes and suspension bridge, was opened on 2 May 1859 and named after the Prince Consort. Brunel was too ill to attend the opening ceremony but was taken across the bridge a few days later, lying on a couch in a railway wagon.

The broad-gauge network spread west into Wales via Gloucester so that by 1845 the company ran trains over more than 246 miles of broad-gauge

This extraordinary-looking locomotive standing outside Exeter St David's shed in 1875 or 1876 was a Bristol & Exeter 4-2-4 tank engine, originally designed by James Pearson. Fitted with 8-foot 10-inch driving wheels, this engine was an 1873 rebuild of a locomotive originally constructed in 1853.

railway. Debates about the merits of the 7-foot gauge had raged from its inception, but plans to extend it north of Oxford via the Oxford, Worcester & Wolverhampton and Banbury & Oxford schemes precipitated what became known as the 'Battle of the Gauges'. To resolve the argument, a Royal Commission was set up in 1846 to investigate the practicality of having a uniform gauge for the whole country. Although the commission eventually

A posed GWR picture of a Brunel timber viaduct at Treviddo in Cornwall.

Gooch 4-2-2 *Sultan*, pictured at Westbourne Park near Paddington. The footplate crew are wearing seemingly impractical cream overalls.

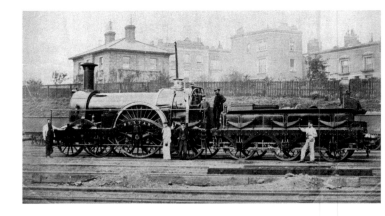

Brunel's magnificent bridge at Saltash, photographed in July 1858 just after being floated into position. It would take a further eight months to jack the bridge up inch by inch and to construct the stone pier.

ruled in favour of Stephenson's standard 4-foot 8½-inch gauge, the broad gauge was not immediately abolished and, although further lines were built, the GWR began to absorb standard-gauge companies.

The acquisition of the Shrewsbury & Chester Railway in 1854 and the leasing of the West Midland Railway five years later added more than 200 miles of standard-gauge track to its network and forced the laying of a third rail on many broad-gauge lines, creating 'mixed' gauge track. Difficult and

expensive to maintain, this arrangement could not continue in the long term, and from 1869 the task of gradually converting the GWR from broad to standard gauge was begun, a process that continued until May 1892, when the last section of the line from Paddington to Penzance was finally converted, ending Brunel's great experiment for good.

An historic picture. The photographer records the passage of the last broad-gauge train in Sonning Cutting near Reading on 21 May 1892. The last train was hauled by a 4-2-2 'Rover' class locomotive.

Broad-gauge aftermath. The sombre scene at Swindon Works after May 1892, with lines of broad-gauge engines awaiting the cutting torch or conversion to standard gauge. The works and the spire of St Mark's church can be seen in the background.

THE GOLDEN AGE
OF THE GWR

A LTHOUGH the end of the broad gauge might have seemed to have been a new beginning for the Great Western, it was not able to shake off the legacy of Brunel immediately. Most contemporary commentators had correctly noted that, while the GWR had been a pioneer when it first opened in 1841, the broad gauge that had made it initially so distinctive had progressively diminished its importance. The sheer cost of conversion, running to several million pounds, even carried out over twenty or so years, crippled the company, starving it of investment and allowing it to fall behind its competitors.

In the twilight years of the broad gauge the GWR had been seized by an inertia triggered by a combination of conservative management and lack of money. Daniel Gooch had become company chairman in 1865, when the railway was close to bankruptcy, and presided over difficult times. The caution and economy practised during those years had a long-term effect on the railway that would take some time to recover from. One writer described the railway as a 'slumbering giant' and it was not until the 1890s that things began to improve significantly. The old order started to change as staff who had begun their careers in the earliest days of the GWR began to retire. One such was G. N. Tyrell, Superintendent of the line until 1888, who was described as 'cautious, anxious, scared of speeds of over 40 mph'. The death of Gooch in 1889 also severed one of the last major links with the era of Brunel.

With new management, ideas and ambition began to permeate the railway at every level. In 1899 J. L. Wilkinson, the company's new General Manager, argued that their aim was to make the GWR 'the biggest railway in every respect in the kingdom ... we want to make our big undertaking *the* undertaking of the country'. Although the GWR had the greatest track mileage of any railway in Britain, it lacked any truly direct route to any town of importance on its network, apart from the Bristol–London main line. Where there were two competing lines, the GWR's route was usually the longer. Its rambling network of lines, combined with its slow trains, led to it being labelled the 'Great Way Round'.

Opposite:
A Churchward 2-8-0 waits at Acton Yard at the head of the first 1000-ton good train in 1913. The large number of different wagons to be seen in the sidings behind the train illustrates the huge variety of goods carried by the company.

The GWR discouraged the travelling public from tipping their staff, as this 1888 notice makes clear.

GREAT WESTERN RAILWAY.

NOTICE.

The Public are requested not to give any Fee to any Porter, Guard, or other Servant of the Company.

HY. LAMBERT,
General Manager.

PADDINGTON, January, 1888.

In the fifteen years before the First World War, the company spent substantial amounts on shortening its route network, which included the construction of entirely new lines. Earlier, in 1886, the opening of the 4-mile Severn Tunnel under the Bristol Channel had been a huge engineering achievement, and allowed the GWR to reduce journey times significantly for both passenger and coal trains to and from South Wales, shortening the route

In 1897 the Great Western Railway provided a grand new royal train for Queen Victoria. She was so attached to her old carriage, built in 1850, that it was incorporated into the new train. The locomotive is *The Queen*, one of William Dean's 'Achilles' Class singles.

Swindon Junction station in the 1890s, just prior to the conversion of the broad gauge. Brunel once wrote to the manager of the infamous refreshment rooms complaining about the quality of the coffee served there, moaning that it tasted of roasted corn.

by 25 miles by cutting out the detour through Gloucester. Matters were improved further with the opening of the Bristol & South Wales Direct Railway in 1903, which linked the Severn Tunnel directly with the original Bristol–London main line at Wootton Bassett near Swindon.

The GWR also invested large sums in the building of 'cut-off' railways, shorter lines bypassing slower sections of existing routes. The construction of cut-offs at Stert and Castle Cary and the upgrading of existing lines such as the Berks & Hants allowed the Great Western to build a new route to the

The English portal of the Severn Tunnel pictured just before opening in 1886, with a contractor's locomotive visible. As if the prospect of keeping out the water of the Bristol Channel was not enough, the tunnel builders also discovered a fresh-water spring deep underground.

A mixture of youth and experience is gathered in front of this Wolverhampton-built GWR '1016' Class 0-6-0 saddle tank. The shunter on the far left of the lineup carries the tool of his trade, a shunter's pole.

West Country which left the old main line at Reading, running parallel to the rival London & South Western route and rejoining the old West Country route near Taunton. All express services to the West of England were switched to this route when it opened in 1906, and the combination of new and old lines enabled trains to avoid Bristol, a notorious bottleneck for trains from Paddington to Devon and Cornwall, and thus cut journey times significantly.

Major changes to lines were matched by dramatic improvements to Great Western train services. Even before the completion of the new West of England route, the GWR had begun to run fast trains on the lucrative 'Ocean Mail' services, carrying mail and disembarking passengers from transatlantic liners to London, in a fierce competition with its rival, the London and South Western Railway (LSWR). The culmination of this rivalry was the run of GWR 4-4-0 locomotive no. 3440 *City of Truro* on 9 May 1904, when it broke the 100-mph mark on Wellington Bank. Amazingly, the news that a Great Western engine had attained a top speed of 102.3 mph was suppressed by the company at the time, fearing that it might frighten the travelling public, and the story was not revealed officially until 1922. A tragic crash at Salisbury on the LSWR in 1906 ended the competition, but the lessons learned by the GWR led to the introduction of further high-speed express services. The 'Cornish Riviera Limited', perhaps the most famous GWR express, was fully inaugurated in 1906 with the opening of the new

Great Western Railway 4-4-0 *City of Truro*, seen at Didcot Railway Centre in 1985. Famous as the first engine to break the 100 mph mark, the locomotive was displayed at Swindon from 1962 to 1984, before being restored to steam again for the 'GW150' celebrations the following year.

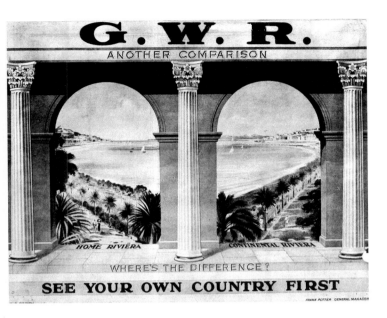

In the years before 1914, the GWR ran an advertising campaign comparing the Cornish Riviera with the French Riviera, arguing that, measured by average temperatures, Cornwall was hotter, and calling on passengers' patriotism to encourage them to stay at home.

West Country route; it ran non-stop to Exeter, with a journey time to Penzance of under seven hours.

These new faster trains were also the result of change at Swindon Works. William Dean had been Locomotive Superintendent since 1877 and had guided the department through difficult times, especially during the long process of gauge conversion. Lack of investment and the impending end of the broad gauge had severely restricted his design output, although his graceful 4-2-2 'Achilles' class and the ultimately long-lived 2301 class, or 'Dean Goods', were very successful engines. By the end of the nineteenth century, pressure of work and the death of two wives and two daughters had taken their toll. The appointment of George Jackson Churchward as Locomotive Superintendent on Dean's retirement in 1902 therefore began a renaissance in locomotive development for the company, and his contribution to the success of the company in this period cannot be underestimated. Churchward had begun his career working for the South Devon Railway in 1873, moving to Swindon when the company was taken over by the GWR, and rising rapidly through the ranks in the works. In 1897 he was appointed assistant to William Dean and the introduction of his pioneering 4-6-0, no. 100,

George Jackson Churchward, Locomotive Superintendent of the GWR from 1902 to 1922. Churchward began his career in 1873 on the South Devon Railway.

Two of William Dean's 'Armstrong' Class 4-4-0s. The rear engine is in its original condition, but the lead locomotive carries a modern taper boiler by Churchward. Even before the end of Dean's tenure as Locomotice Superintendent the ideas that would put his successor's designs at the forefront were being put into practice.

Churchward's 'Saint' class *Viscount Churchill*. These locomotives were among the most advanced, and beautiful, to be designed before the First World War.

months before Dean's retirement marked the beginning of a revolution in design that was not only to dominate Great Western locomotive policy for the next forty years, but also to influence the designs of many other railways, such as the London Midland and Scottish.

Until the Edwardian era, express services on the GWR had been hauled by Dean 4-2-2 and 4-4-0 designs, but the success of no. 100 led to the introduction of the very successful two-cylinder 4-6-0 'Saint' class engines, followed closely by the more powerful four-cylinder 'Star' class in 1907, which rapidly took over all long-distance passenger services on the railway.

A coloured postcard view of no. 104, one of the 'Frenchmen' purchased by the Great Western in 1905. This locomotive was later named *Alliance*.

These designs were so successful and influential that they formed the basis of later Collett express engines such as the 'Castle' and 'King' classes built in the 1920s.

Although standardisation had been introduced by Daniel Gooch as early as the 1840s, Churchward fully developed the idea, producing a range of locomotive designs including 2-6-2 tank engines, and 2-6-0 and 2-8-0 freight engines, all fitted with many interchangeable standard parts such as boilers, cylinders, cab fittings and valve gear.

Although Churchward and his team built powerful and free-steaming engines that were steeped in GWR tradition, he was not afraid to investigate and use innovations developed elsewhere, especially in France and the United States, purchasing three De Glehn compound locomotives from France to test against his own engines. Nor was progress confined to the locomotive works: the clerestory carriage, a familiar sight on the railway in the nineteenth century, was gradually replaced by more modern designs, such as the 'Dreadnought' and 'Toplight' carriages, which had corridors and toilets.

GWR 4-6-2 no. 111 *The Great Bear*, built in 1908. Churchward's design was the only 'Pacific' to be produced by the company. The engine was too heavy for most routes and spent most of its life on the Bristol–London main line before being rebuilt into a 'Castle' Class locomotive in 1924.

By the beginning of the First World War, railway workers at Swindon could call on a range of social facilities. As well as a cradle-to-grave health service, the GWR Medical Fund, they could visit the Mechanics' Institute, seen here in the 1920s, the home of many recreational clubs and societies and a large theatre.

New sleeping carriages and restaurant cars were also introduced on long-distance trains, greatly improving conditions for passengers.

To produce all these designs, Churchward also oversaw the transformation of the works at Swindon. By 1914 the factory employed twelve thousand staff, and considerable sums had been spent in re-equipping the workshops with the facilities to allow them to build new engines and rolling stock to the highest standards. In contrast to the outdated facilities built during the broad-gauge era, workshops constructed after 1900 were modern and equipped with the most up-to-date machinery. A new 230,000-square-foot erecting shop was built before the outbreak of war in 1914, but a larger extension to what became known as the 'A' Shop was not finally completed until 1920. This completed a process of redevelopment that left Swindon at the forefront of railway engineering in Britain and the wider railway world.

The new steel roof span at Paddington station, which was based on Brunel's original designs, nears completion in 1913.

Gerrards Cross station on the newly improved GWR route to Birmingham. The platforms were used mainly for local trains, like the two steam railmotors seen in this picture. Non-stop two-hour expresses between London and the second city used the two middle tracks.

Passengers queue at one of the booking offices at Birmingham Snow Hill station not long after its rebuilding in 1913. The station was demolished in the 1970s, but trains now run through a new station on the site.

In order to escape from the dark days of the broad gauge, the railway also spent large amounts on passenger facilities. Brunel's great terminus at Paddington was updated and expanded in 1913 by the construction of an additional roof span, duplicating the work of the great engineer, but built with steel rather than wrought iron.

The GWR also spent almost £1 million on the reconstruction of its station in Birmingham. Before rebuilding, Snow Hill station was cramped, grubby and congested, and hardly an advertisement for a company

Three young GWR porters pose for a picture at Paddington, later reproduced on a postcard issued in the years before the First World War. Behind them is one of the company's patriotic 'See Your Own Country First' posters.

27

The GWR was an early pioneer in the operation of bus services acting as feeders for areas not directly served by their stations. This 1904 poster advertises a route linking small Wiltshire villages between the company's Calne and Marlborough branches.

taking such trouble to improve its services and lines. The new station was almost double the size of the old one, and the task of demolishing the existing structure and building the new one took more than seven years. By 1913 the new station was complete, ready to receive trains running express services from London in two hours, directly competing with the London and North Western Railway. Journey times had been improved by further work on the Paddington–Birmingham line, shortening the route by 18 miles.

The GWR also built new halts in rural and urban locations to attract additional passengers; many of these stations were served by steam 'rail motors' built to compete with trams and buses. The company was also the first railway to operate bus feeder services from its stations and in 1903 it began running 'road motors' from Helston to the Lizard in Cornwall. By 1920 it was running a fleet of 130 buses.

Another significant development in the years before 1914 was the construction of a new deep-water port at Fishguard in West Wales, a project costing almost £1 million. The company had also purchased new fast steamships to operate between Fishguard and the Irish port of Rosslare. Although initial plans were aimed at building a harbour to serve the lucrative Irish cross-channel traffic, it became apparent that the railway had ambitious ideas for Fishguard after its opening in 1906. When the liner

Another means of attracting business to the railway was the running of special excursion trains, often to the coast. This photograph shows passengers at Holt station in Wiltshire awaiting an excursion train to Portsmouth in 1905.

Mauretania called at the port in 1908, the GWR was hoping that Fishguard might become a rival to Liverpool or Plymouth in attracting transatlantic liner traffic, but this prospect was dashed by the outbreak of the First World War.

The period of sustained expansion and development on the Great Western was brought to a dramatic halt by the First World War and the centralised government control of railways by the Railway Executive, although there were signs that GWR shareholders were becoming restless at the sheer scale of investment put into the expansion of the company and the consequent effect on their dividends.

When German U-boats made the movement of coal by sea impossible, it was left to the railways to carry it. More than 80 per cent of the coal used

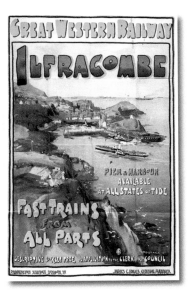

Produced in the Edwardian era, this GWR poster features one of the paddle steamers that plied the route between the north coast of Devon and Somerset and South Wales.

Fishguard Harbour pictured in 1906. Thousands of tons of rocks were removed from the cliffs, to allow construction of the station, dock and other facilities. GWR steamships used on the route to Rosslare in Ireland sit alongside the dock awaiting departure.

by the British fleet was steam coal from South Wales, and millions of tons were transported by the GWR to Warrington, from where trains were sent on to Grangemouth in Scotland. By 1918, an average of seventy-nine trains carrying 32,000 tons of coal were being worked by the company each week; by the end of the war this figure had been exceeded, the highest total being 56,000 tons in one week. Trains were also worked through the Severn Tunnel towards Swindon and the east coast.

Apart from the thousands of troop trains run during the war, the GWR also handled more than six thousand loaded ambulance trains from south coast ports to locations all over the network. Of these services, 2,848 stopped at Great Western stations to unload sick and wounded troops from the Western Front, with Bristol Temple Meads bearing the brunt of this work, closely followed by Paddington, Cardiff and Plymouth.

The works at Swindon undertook work for the War Office, the Ministry of Munitions and the Admiralty. The skill and adaptability of the staff at the factory was proved by the huge variety of tasks they tackled, often at short notice. Two of the best-known tasks were the preparation of a number of 'Dean Goods' and ex-Great Central Railway 2-8-0 locomotives for service overseas and the conversion or construction of 238 carriages for ambulance train use.

The special canteen set up at Paddington to cater for the thousands of service personnel travelling on the GWR during the First World War.

An enormous range of other work was carried out. It included the manufacture of Hotchkiss guns, various large gun carriages, shell parts, shells, bombs and other ammunition components. The Carriage and Wagon Department also built wagons, water carts, stretchers and many other smaller items. Although the contribution made to the war effort was vital, the normal maintenance regime for GWR locomotives was disrupted and after the war standards dropped – a situation that would take some years to rectify.

Although employment on the railway was designated as a 'reserved occupation' during the conflict, more and more men were conscripted as the war dragged on. By 1919, 25,479 had joined up, 32 per cent of the railway's pre-war establishment. The loss of so many staff was felt intensely by the GWR and during the course of the war it employed large numbers of women. By August 1918, 6,345 were working for the company.

With the end of the conflict, the GWR counted the human cost of the 'war to end all wars'. By 1919, 2,436 employees had been killed and many more injured. The Locomotive Department had been particularly hard hit, with 825 casualties, and at Swindon Works virtually every workshop had its own war memorial.

Platform 1 at Paddington was the scene of a sombre ceremony on Armistice Day, 11 November 1920, when wreaths were laid by GWR staff in memory of those killed during the First World War.

CRICCIETH

THE CAERNARVONSHIRE RESORT FACING SOUTH

IDEAL SUMMER AND WINTER CLIMATE

GUIDE AND ACCOMMODATION LIST FROM SECRETARY
INFORMATION BUREAU, CRICCIETH

PRINTED IN GREAT BRITAIN BY LOWE & BRYDONE PRINTERS LTD, LONDON, N.W.10.

THE GREATER GREAT WESTERN

THE PROCESS of recovering from the First World War was a gradual one, and after 1919 the railway, like the country, was short of investment with which to restore its trains, stations and lines to pre-war standards. Time was also needed to recruit new staff to fill the gaps left by those killed or injured. Despite the war, the Great Western still found itself in a strong position by comparison with some of its rivals; it owned and operated more than 3,000 miles of line, on which there were more than 1,100 stations, ranging from very large ones, such as Paddington and Birmingham Snow Hill, to tiny halts or country stations. To operate this great empire, the GWR had more than seventy thousand staff and over three thousand locomotives, eight thousand passenger vehicles and a staggering 78,000 goods and mineral wagons. In addition, there was an extensive fleet of horse-drawn and motor road vehicles, a large shipping fleet and important hotels such as the Great Western Royal Hotel at Paddington and the Tregenna Castle Hotel at St Ives.

Before the Railways Act of 1921 there were more than a hundred separate railway companies in Britain; in the years after the war their combined deficit was a staggering £41 million and increasing. The success of the Railway Executive, which controlled Britain's railways during the First World War, led the government to consider full-scale nationalisation but this was rejected in favour of the amalgamation of railways into four large companies, each serving a different sector of the country.

It was not surprising, therefore, that the Great Western was seen as the dominant force in the 'western group' of the new 'Big Four' companies, and initially the GWR directors argued that it should be the only constituent of the new grouping, with all other railways being absorbed. This proposal was disputed by some of the larger Welsh lines such as the Barry and Taff Vale companies, which argued that their dividends of 10 per cent had been higher than that paid to GWR shareholders on occasions. As a result, the enlarged Great Western Railway that came into being on 1 January 1922 consisted of the original GWR company and six other 'constituents':

Opposite:
The GWR commissioned many of the best poster artists to produce designs for its advertising material between the two world wars. This striking poster for the Welsh resort of Criccieth was by Albert Lambart, who also produced posters for the LMS and LNER.

Alexandra (Newport & South
Wales) Docks and Railway

Barry Railway

Cambrian Railway

Cardiff Railway

Rhymney Railway

Taff Vale Railway

In addition, a further group of 'subsidiary' railways were also absorbed into the new railway over the next eighteen months. These included:

Brecon & Merthyr Railway

Burry Port and Gwendraeth
Railway

Cleobury Mortimer & Ditton
Priors Light Railway

Didcot Newbury &
Southampton

Exeter Central

Forest of Dean Central

Gwendraeth Valleys Railway

Lampeter, Aberayron & New Quay

Liskeard & Looe

Llanelly & Mynydd Mawr
Railway

Mawddwy

Midland & South Western
Junction Railway

Neath & Brecon Railway

Penarth Extension

Penarth Harbour Dock &
Railway

Port Talbot Railway

Princetown

Rhondda & Swansea Bay Railway

Ross & Monmouth

South Wales Mineral Railway

Swansea Harbour Trust

Teign Valley

Vale of Glamorgan

Welshpool & Llanfair

West Somerset

Wrexham & Ellesmere

It seemed that the Great Western was the only company to escape from the painful process of the Grouping relatively unscathed. A satirical cartoon appeared in the *South Wales Echo* in November 1922; headed 'A Survival of Title', it showed a member of the GWR staff saying 'Hooray! Never even blew me cap off', with a caption noting: 'None of the companies which

By the time of the Grouping in 1923, the Taff Vale Railway had nearly three hundred locomotives in its fleet. Many, like this example, no. 68, were of the 0-6-2 type, a wheel arrangement that was most common in South Wales. At the Grouping, 446 of the 767 engines belonging to South Wales railways absorbed by the GWR were of this type.

survive the amalgamation upheaval have come out of it with such enhanced prestige.' While the Great Western inheritance was considerable, and some of the larger Welsh companies remained fiercely independent, many of the smaller companies had been operated by the Great Western for many years, thus reducing the disruption and upset of the reorganisation.

It was no coincidence that a Welsh newspaper should pay attention to the Grouping, since the six largest constituent companies joining the GWR were situated in the region. Apart from the Cambrian Railway, they covered a large area of South Wales and carried predominantly coal; the oldest, the Taff Vale Railway, was only a year younger than the GWR.

THE GREAT WESTERN · "Hooray! Never even blew me cap off!"

A satirical cartoon for the *South Wales Echo* newspaper commenting in 1922 on the fact that the GWR had emerged relatively unscathed from the creation of the 'Big Four' companies.

The most significant consequence of the addition of these South Wales railways to the GWR portfolio was that it made the company the largest dock-owner in the world. By operating ports at Cardiff, Swansea, Newport, Barry, Penarth and Port Talbot, the company took on a lucrative business that handled more than 50 million tons of goods a year, of which 75 per cent was coal shifted from mines in the South Wales valleys. The remaining 25 per cent included practically every kind of commodity imported or exported

Newport Docks in the 1920s, with Scandinavian pit-prop timbers being unloaded from the SS *Tvedestrand* before being moved by rail to coal mines in the valleys. A wagon belonging to the Neath & Brecon Railway, closest to the camera, indicates that the picture was taken shortly after Grouping.

into Great Britain. As well as coal, steel rail and plate, petrol and other chemicals were exported, while pig iron, timber, flour, fish, vegetables, meat and other foodstuffs were imported.

In contrast, the remaining constituent company, the Cambrian, was very different. Much of its rambling 300-mile network was single-track and ran through difficult terrain in rural Wales; its 2,358 staff were scattered over a wide area. Of the smaller, subsidiary companies absorbed by the GWR, the majority were located either in Wales or the borders, and most were small independent lines that even by 1921 were struggling to survive. Two further cross-country routes made up the group, the Didcot Newbury & Southampton Railway and the Midland & South Western Junction Railway.

In the years after Grouping this inheritance seemed to be a big asset to the GWR. To speed the handling and dispatch of coal at its ports, in 1923 the company invested heavily in the introduction of 20-ton steel coal wagons to transport coal from pit to port, replacing thousands of ancient wooden 10-ton wagons. Colliery owners gladly accepted this innovation, along with improvements to equipment at the docks costing almost £2 million. The optimism was short-lived as coal production slumped in 1925, precipitating pay cuts and redundancies for staff.

Although Great Western staff and management had come to an unpalatable agreement in these difficult times, the same could not be said for coal owners and miners, and when the recommendations of a Royal Commission were rejected by miners a strike seemed inevitable. Given the links between railway unions and miners, it was not surprising that the GWR was drawn into what became known as the General Strike, which began on 3 May 1926. Although the company was able to run increasing numbers of trains as the dispute dragged on, in many areas support remained solid, and the repercussions would last long after the end of the strike on 14 May, with bad feeling existing between those who went on strike and those who remained at work continuing long after the Second World War in some places. More significant was that while railway workers returned to work miners did not, and mines remained

As well as the more glamorous express services such as the 'Cornish Riviera Limited', the GWR ran thousands of excursions. This handbill advertises a trip from Bristol stations to the capital in January 1926.

Great Western Railway.

THE OPPORTUNITY TO VISIT YOUR FRIENDS.

On SUNDAY, February 7th
AN EXPRESS HALF-DAY EXCURSION
WILL RUN TO

LONDON

RETURN FARES, THIRD CLASS.	LEAVING	AT	RETURN FARES, THIRD CLASS.
From Bristol Stations **6/-**	BRISTOL	a.m.	From Bristol Stations **6/-**
	Bedminster	11 0	
	Temple Meads	11 10	
	Clifton Down	10 40	
	Montpelier	10 45	
	Stapleton Road	10 50	
	Lawrence Hill	10 55	
From BATH **5/6**	BATH	11 30	From SWINDON **5/-**
	SWINDON	p.m. 12 15	
	PADDINGTON arr.	1 52	

The RETURN TRAIN will leave PADDINGTON STATION at 9.20 p.m. the same day.

TICKETS IN ADVANCE. It will assist the Company in the provision of accommodation if intending passengers will obtain their tickets in advance.

PASSENGERS SHOULD RETAIN THIS HANDBILL FOR REFERENCE TO ENSURE TRAVELLING BY THE SPECIFIED TRAINS IN EACH DIRECTION

N.B.—The tickets will not be available for the return journey unless presented to and nipped by the ticket examiner on the outward journey.

Children under Three years of age, Free ; Three and under Twelve, Half-price. No luggage allowed. Excursion tickets are only available to and from the stations named upon them. Should an Excursion ticket be used for any other station than those named upon it, or by any other train than as specified herein, it will be rendered void, and therefore the fare paid will be liable to forfeiture and the full Ordinary Fare will become chargeable.

Tickets available for return on day of issue only. The tickets are not transferable. Tickets in advance may be obtained at all Booking Stations and the undermentioned Offices :—
BRISTOL—
Tickets can be obtained in advance at the G.W.R. Offices, 3 High Street, City ; "Pickford's" Office, St. Augustine's Parade ; at 25 Baldwin Street, City (Messrs. T. Cook & Son, Ltd.) ; at Mr. H. W. Cooper's Office, 2 Cromwell Road, Montpelier (Zetland Road Junction) ; at the Polytechnic Lewins Association, 14 Bridge Street, City ; "Sloan's" Library, 5 and 5 New Station Road, Fishponds ; at the G.W.R. Offices, Regent Street, Kingswood ; 68 Redcliffe Street ; 10 Portland Place and 35a Queen's Road, Clifton ; 17 Pritchard Street, Portland Square, and Gloucester Road, Avonmouth.
BATH—
G.W.R. Offices, 22 New Bond Street, or Messrs. W. W. Bell & Co., 7 New Bond Street.
For any further information respecting the arrangements shown in this bill, application should be made at any of the Company's Offices or Agencies ; to Mr. H. R. Griffiths, Divisional Superintendent, Bristol ; or to Mr. R. H. Nicholls, Superintendent of the Line, Paddington Station, London, W.2.

Paddington Station.   **FELIX J. C. POLE,**
January, 1926.   *General Manager.*

(Bristol 15,500)   Burleigh Ltd., Printers and Lithographers, Lewin's Mead, Bristol.   (B7/79)

closed until the winter of 1926, with severe consequences for the GWR. Coal traffic dropped by 20 million tons that year, and by 1930 the amount of coal it moved was still below pre-war levels.

To make matters worse, the GWR began to experience increasing levels of competition from road transport. The extensive use of lorries during the war had proved their worth, and many soldiers returning from the conflict set up their own haulage businesses. To compete, the existing country lorry service was expanded in the 1920s, although its impact was limited. More significant was the introduction of a rural railhead distribution service. Specialised collection and delivery contracts were agreed with large customers guaranteeing delivery times, usually within a 30-mile radius of larger stations, and by 1930 over 1,300 lorries were operated by the company.

Although the financial position of the company did improve, the Wall Street Crash of October 1929 again made it difficult for the GWR to generate business. Short of capital, it took advantage of government assistance in the form of the 1929 Development (Loan Guarantees and Grants) Act, which made finance available in return for schemes that would alleviate unemployment. There had

A copy of the *British Worker*, issued by the Trades Union Congress on the third day of the General Strike in 1926.

Some idea of the sheer scale of the Great Western's coal business in South Wales can be seen in this 1920s photograph of one of the large marshalling yards outside Newport.

37

A striking publicity picture, featuring the most famous GWR locomotive of all, no. 6000 *King George V*, at the entrance to Middle Hill Tunnel near Box in 1927.

been little major investment on the GWR since the war, and the £4.5 million made available was used to tackle all manner of major projects. Passenger facilities at Paddington, Bristol Temple Meads, Taunton and Cardiff Central were extended and updated, and further improvements were made to the West of England main line by the construction of avoiding lines at Frome and Westbury. More dramatic was the provision of a new flyover at Cogload Junction, where the route joined the Bristol–Exeter line. Less glamorous

plans were made to extend marshalling yards at Banbury, Rogerstone and Severn Tunnel Junction, as well as improving engine shed facilities at locations all over the network.

As early as 1923 the GWR had scored a major public relations coup with the introduction of its 'Castle' Class locomotives, their introduction being accompanied by a vigorous publicity drive. With a tractive effort of 31,625 pounds, they were billed as 'the most powerful locomotives in the country'. It was also arranged that the first of the class, *Caerphilly Castle*, should appear next to Nigel Gresley's new A1 'Pacific' at the British Empire Exhibition in 1924, its diminutive appearance causing further debate when it was revealed that it was more powerful than the LNER design.

Caerphilly Castle was the first major design to be produced at Swindon under C. B. Collett, who had been appointed as Chief Mechanical Engineer of the GWR in 1922 following the retirement of G. J. Churchward. In the following twenty years, Collett went on to produce many of the engines now seen as 'classic' GWR designs. Despite the difficulties suffered by the company between the wars, the era was a high point for steam traction, and the Great Western was able to run some of the fastest and most famous expresses in the world.

More importantly, the Great Western publicity machine developed under General Manager Felix Pole in the 1920s grew ever more sophisticated and better able to promote the railway and its services in Britain and abroad. After Pole's retirement in 1929, his replacement, Sir James Milne, modernised the company's publicity material, introducing the now familiar GWR 'shirt-button' monogram and adopting the use of Gill Sans typeface, as well as issuing posters and other publicity material.

Much company publicity was concentrated on the promotion of the West Country and was largely responsible for the development of the 'Cornish Riviera' as a

Craftsmen at Swindon Works produced more than the locomotives, carriages and wagons it was famous for. This picture shows an artificial hand and foot made for unfortunate GWR staff injured in shunting accidents on the railway in the 1930s.

In April 1924 Swindon Works received a royal visit from King George V and Queen Mary. The visit included a footplate ride on no. 4082 *Windsor Castle*, and the Queen has been helpfully provided with a cloth to keep her hands free of grease or soot.

One of the most famous publicity pictures issued by the Great Western Railway shows seven of its new 'King' Class express locomotives grouped together outside Swindon's running shed. To be seen are nos. 6005, 6008, 6017, 6020, 6022, 6023 and 6024.

Taking tea from one of the company's refreshment trolleys at Paddington in the 1930s.

holiday destination. Through imaginative and striking posters, the company promoted Cornwall, Devon and other holiday areas and also produced such publications as the annual *Holiday Haunts*, a book that featured not only information on GWR train services, but also details of hotels, boarding houses and other accommodation for holidaymakers. The company also issued a series of very popular jigsaws featuring locations on the railway, now avidly collected by enthusiasts.

Between the wars, the GWR publicity department could also boast that it operated the world's fastest train. This was the 'Cheltenham Flyer', which from 1929 averaged 66.2 mph over the 77-mile stretch from Swindon to Paddington, making it the fastest scheduled train in the world. By 1932 the average speed had been increased to over 70 mph; a specially staged run in June that year resulted in an average of 81.7 mph, a figure just beaten by the LNER 'Coronation' train five years later. By the Second World War high-speed services in Europe and the United States had snatched away the record for good.

The GWR also heavily publicised the introduction of another new venture in 1934 when diesel railcars were brought into service. Initially the company used single-car streamlined railcars built by the AEC Company. Their sleek shape and Art Deco design made them popular with travellers, and they were used on services between Cardiff and Birmingham. A second, later batch of vehicles was produced at Swindon Works with a more angular body design and running gear more suitable for work on branch lines, where it was hoped they might be a more economic alternative to steam traction.

Apart from suspension during both world wars, the *Holiday Haunts* book was produced by the GWR annually from 1904 to 1948. As well as descriptions of areas served by the railway, it featured advertising for hotels, boarding houses and other accommodation at holiday resorts.

Apart from interruptions for war, the GWR produced thousands of copies of *Holiday Haunts* each year, advertising holiday resorts served by the railway.

A crowd gathers on platform 1 of Paddington station, where a train is waiting to take it to the delights of the West Country, some time in the 1920s.

The GWR reached its centenary in 1935 and although there had been events to mark the centenaries of both the Stockton & Darlington and Liverpool & Manchester railways, the chance to celebrate its hundredth birthday was an ideal opportunity for the GWR to strike a blow against its rivals and publicise its services to the public. A BBC radio programme was broadcast and a special film produced that featured footage of the railway in 1935 and specially staged reconstructions of key moments in Great Western history.

The GWR also used its birthday to launch two new ventures that typified the drive of the railway during the period. The first was the introduction of a new express train, the 'Bristolian', a non-stop service between Paddington and Bristol Temple Meads, leaving the capital at 4.30 p.m. With a journey time of $1^3\square_4$ hours the new train was fifteen minutes faster than existing trains. The second development in centenary year was the replacement of carriages on the 'Cornish Riviera Limited' with brand new 'Centenary Stock', just as luxurious as Pullman carriages, and showing that the GWR continued to offer high-quality express travel for its passengers despite all the trials and tribulations it had endured since the Grouping.

The press launch of the GWR's new diesel railcar on 1 December 1933, with the AEC-produced vehicle standing on platform 2 next to the more conventional lines of a 'King' Class engine.

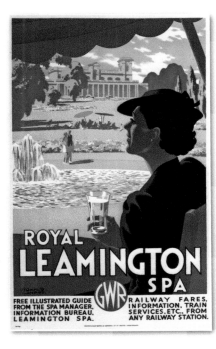

An evocative Art Deco style poster produced in the 1930s to advertise Leamington Spa.

THE GREAT WESTERN
UNDER ATTACK

THE GREAT WESTERN had done all it could to recover from the effects of the economic depression and, while business had been good in 1938, the uncertain international situation following the Munich Crisis that year had caused revenue to drop by almost £2 million in 1939. When the Second World War began on 3 September 1939, the Big Four companies and London Transport were effectively nationalised, coming under the control of the Railway Executive Committee, as they had been in the First World War.

The first major task undertaken by the GWR was the evacuation of almost 113,000 schoolchildren from London and other major urban areas to safer locations in the countryside in the days before the declaration of war. Although evacuation plans had been prepared well in advance by company staff, the railway nevertheless had only twenty-four hours to implement an urgent government request and the first trains left Paddington at 8.30 a.m. on 1 September 1939. Over the next four days, thousands of children were moved from the London, Birmingham and Liverpool areas to locations all over the West Country and Wales. Further evacuation trains were run by the company during the height of the Blitz; in February 1941 more than seven thousand children were evacuated from the Bristol area to Cornwall and Devon.

The war stretched the GWR to its limits and beyond, with the number of passengers carried increasing dramatically; in the early days of the war it moved thousands of 'unofficial' evacuees fleeing cities for safer rural locations. Not surprisingly, holiday trains were suspended for the duration, and expresses such as the 'Cornish Riviera Limited' curtailed. To replace this business, the GWR had to cope with far greater numbers of military personnel travelling to and from bases all over the network and increasing numbers of war workers commuting to and from munitions establishments. An illustration of just how much traffic increased was that in 1939 the GWR issued over 84,000 tickets for travel. This figure had grown to over 147,000 in 1944, with only a slight decrease the following year.

The scale and strategic nature of the Great Western Railway made it a target for enemy bombing, with most of the major stations on the system

Opposite:
A female GWR worker pastes up one of the most famous Second World War 'Home Front' posters at Paddington.

Evacuees leaving Bristol Stapleton Road station in 1941 for resorts in Devon and Cornwall.

GREAT WESTERN RAILWAY

SUMMER TRIPS

through ninety miles of Thames Scenery

OXFORD to KINGSTON

Saloon Steamers run daily
Sundays included, between
Oxford, Wallingford, Henley
Windsor, Kingston

May 25th to Sept. 17th, 1939

For Further particulars see Steamer Guide
and Time Table — Post Free Threepence

SALTER BROS., LTD.
FOLLY BRIDGE, TEL. 2421 and 2899   OXFORD

PLEASE   KEEP   FOR   REFERENCE

No doubt this handbill advertising trips on the Thames was quickly forgotten with the onset of the 'Phoney War' after war was declared on 3 September 1939.

Right: A company air-raid shelter at Ealing in 1939. The GWR employee, a member of the ARP, has also donned his helmet and gas mask for the photographer.

damaged in air raids, particularly during the Blitz in 1940 and 1941. The company had spent much time and effort on extensive air-raid precautions and blackout measures; many staff joined Air Raid Precautions or Home Guard units to help in the war effort but the ferocity and frequency of air raids inevitably led to considerable damage and casualties. Hard hit were the company's docks in South Wales, and stations and goods depots in Bristol,

The offices at Birmingham Snow Hill are heavily sandbagged in this wartime view.

Birmingham, Newton Abbot, Plymouth and London. Only two locomotives were destroyed by enemy action, a 4-6-0, *Bowden Hall*, in 1941 and an 0-6-0 pannier tank, no. 1729, hit in a raid on Castle Cary in 1942.

Travelling by train in the blackout was a difficult proposition for staff and passengers alike, and blacked-out carriages, low train speeds and the removal of station name-boards and lighting made life particularly hard. Conditions for

A direct hit on the 7.10 p.m. Bristol to Salisbury train as it left Bristol Temple Meads station on 6 December 1940 resulted in the death of the driver of Churchward 'Mogul' no. 4358 and fifteen passengers.

GREAT WESTERN RAILWAY

Notice to Passengers

Passengers are advised to take shelter during an Air Raid and not to remain on the station platforms, where there may be a serious risk of danger from falling glass and splinters.

August, 1940.

J. MILNE,

General Manager.

Many stations had large glass roofs over their platforms, making them very dangerous places in air raids.

locomotive crews were especially tough. Engine cabs were blacked out with a combination of steel plating over windows and tarpaulins masking the glow of the locomotive firebox. It was not, however, always possible to exclude all light from the engine, making trains an easy target for enemy aircraft at night.

In South Wales, the GWR docks played a vital role in the war effort, largely by dramatically changing their function. The war had considerably reduced the output and export of coal, and ports found themselves importing and exporting more general cargoes, particularly foodstuffs and other imports brought across by Atlantic convoy. As the war progressed, the dock facilities increasingly became a major centre for the import and storage of munitions and equipment for the planned invasion of Europe by the Allies. The GWR steamship fleet was also pressed into action, with a number of ships playing a key role in the evacuation of British troops at Dunkirk, and also assisting in later campaigns.

At Swindon, much of the works was turned over to war work and only the minimum of maintenance was carried out on its own locomotives and rolling stock. The construction programme was reduced for the duration. Among the locomotives that were built during this period were a number for the War Department, including LMS-designed Stanier 2-8-0 '8F' goods engines. The works also refurbished one hundred elderly 'Dean Goods' locomotives that had been requisitioned by the War Department for use overseas and also built carriages for ambulance trains used both at home and

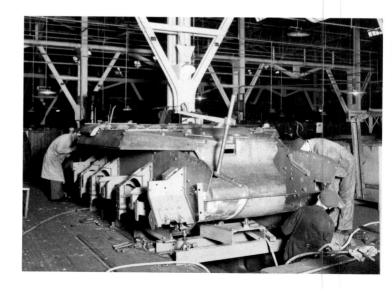

Swindon Works staff at work building a 25-ton tank in 1941. The work was carried out in artificial light even in daylight hours since the glass rooflights had been painted over to create a blackout.

in Europe. The adaptable and inventive Swindon workforce was also called on to produce all manner of equipment for the forces, including landing craft, midget submarines and gun mountings, as well as thousands of bombs and shells.

Above all, the war had the greatest effect on the GWR staff. While many were employed in reserved occupations, by the end of the conflict more than 15,000 Great Western staff were serving in the forces or in full-time civil defence. Although staff levels increased by more than twelve thousand to compensate, the most significant problem for the GWR was the loss of skilled staff; many of the jobs vacated had involved years of training and could not easily be filled overnight. Many of the replacement staff were women, more than sixteen thousand of whom were employed all over the railway, working as ticket collectors, guards, porters and workshop staff at Swindon.

In the months before and after the Allied invasion of Europe in 1944 money spent on upgrading the GWR network over the years proved vital, along with further investment in upgrading two cross-country lines, the old Midland & South Western Junction and Didcot Newbury & Southampton railways, into major routes. Both these lines linked Channel ports with the Midlands and the north of England and handled thousands of troop and munitions trains in the course of the campaign.

A female boilersmith drills the firebox of a GWR locomotive boiler. In common with her male counterparts, she wears little in the way of ear protection in one of the noisiest workshops in the factory.

Keeping on: a Great Western guard signals the 'right away' for his train at Paddington in 1940.

GREAT WESTERN RAILWAY.

EXPLOSIVES

3

PLACE AS FAR
AS PRACTICABLE
FROM ENGINE,
BRAKE-VAN AND
VEHICLES
LABELLED
"INFLAMMABLE."

DATE _____ 19__ TRAIN
FROM _____
TO _____
VIA _____
SHEETS IN or ON Wagon, Total No.___
Owner and No. of Wagon.___
Consignee _____

**SHUNT
WITH
GREAT
CARE.**

LOAD AND UNLOAD
OUTSIDE
GOODS SHEDS.

This label to be used for **GUNPOWDER** and all other **EXPLOSIVES.**

The GWR had always transported dangerous and explosive materials such as gunpowder but during the war carried enormous amounts of munitions. This wagon label instructs staff to place explosives wagons 'as far as practicable from the engine'.

As the invasion progressed, staff also dealt with a steady stream of ambulance trains, handling 142 in June 1944 alone.

Despite Allied successes, further pressure was placed on the Great Western in June and July 1944 when German V1 bombs began to rain down on the capital and other British cities. As well as official evacuation trains, the company also had to cope with thousands of other travellers desperate to flee the capital. The situation was so bad on 29 July that the company was forced to close Paddington station for three hours when it became completely choked by thousands of people. The situation was only averted when the Prime Minister's Office allowed an extra sixty-three trains to be run to relieve the congestion. Within a year, further additional trains were required for recently 'demobbed' service staff when the conflict ended, and the company began to look forward to its recovery. At the first post-war annual general meeting of the company, the chairman, Viscount Portal, conceded that the GWR had much to do to restore pre-war standards and to begin again the programme of locomotive and carriage renewal it abandoned in 1939.

In the years following the end of hostilities the GWR lived under the shadow of nationalisation. Even before 1945, there had been considerable discussions about the future of Britain's railways in peacetime. The success of the Railway Executive during the war was clearly a key factor but cynical observers also noted that the railways that had struggled before the war were now most supportive of the idea of nationalisation. This view was not shared by the directors and management of the GWR, who were firmly opposed to any idea of nationalised control of the railway.

Despite the determination of its staff to recover from the war, the Great Western's efforts to re-establish itself were badly affected by the period of extreme austerity endured in Britain in the aftermath of the war. Raw materials, staff and vital investment were in short supply and the company was even forced to reintroduce salvage drives, a measure adopted during the darkest years of the war.

The most difficult issue was the shortage of coal, made worse by the extreme winter of 1946–7. Icy spells in December 1946 were followed by prolonged cold weather that lasted from January to March 1947. With temperatures below freezing, an already weakened Britain ground to a halt, with many trains delayed not only by snowdrifts on the line, but also when Arctic conditions caused brakes and water troughs to freeze solid. Coal was stuck at mines and, when it could be shifted, its quality was often variable. Some imported coal was available, but its quality did not suit GWR engines designed to run on Welsh steam coal.

American troops at Cardiff Docks, boarding ships bound for France shortly before D-Day in 1944.

As well as tanks and troops, the war effort needed fuel, and the company transported millions of gallons of petrol, particularly in the months before D-Day. Here a GWR train leaves a depot 'somewhere in England', bound for a Channel port.

With coal in short supply, and also double its pre-war price, Great Western management made strenuous efforts to find new types of fuel to run their trains. In 1938 the GWR had carried out work on the possibility of electrifying the main lines west of Taunton but had not proceeded with the idea. Already operating a fleet of railcars, the GWR then placed an order for seventeen diesel shunting locomotives, with diesel oil seemingly easier to obtain.

Pride in the job: Driver Moore oils the moving parts of GWR 'Castle' Class locomotive *Earl of Radnor* in 1946.

A bolder move was the conversion of steam locomotives to run on oil. Trials were carried out using twenty 2-8-0 freight engines and, once the technology had been tested, the scheme was extended to include eleven 'Hall' and five 'Castle' Class passenger locomotives. It seemed initially that the scheme might be extended further as the locomotives steamed well, and the lack of ash and clinker to clean from fireboxes was welcomed by engine-shed staff. Government hopes that by converting more than a thousand locomotives on all 'Big Four' lines it could reduce coal consumption by more than a million tons a year were dashed when difficulties in maintaining supplies of fuel and its cost led to the scheme being abandoned. All the modified GWR engines were converted back to coal by 1950.

A more unconventional choice of motive power was made by the GWR in 1946 when it ordered a gas turbine locomotive from the Swiss firm of Brown Boveri, and, with nationalisation looming, the company ordered another from the British Metropolitan Vickers company. They were not delivered until 1950 and 1951 respectively and, as well as being expensive to run, spent much time at Swindon Works under repair before being withdrawn after a relatively short working life. Swindon tradition did, however, continue, notwithstanding these experiments and the retirement of C. B. Collett in 1942. Collett's

The press launch and inaugural run of F. W. Hawksworth's 'County' Class locomotive no. 1000 *County of Middlesex* in 1945. These two-cylinder engines were powerful and well-liked by locomotive crews.

successor was F. W. Hawksworth, another GWR stalwart, who had little opportunity during the war years to develop locomotive design very far. After 1945, lack of resources meant that he was able to produce only one major new passenger design, the 4-6-0 'County' Class, and a modernised pannier-tank design, as well as supervising the construction of further 'Castle' and 'Hall' Class engines, which, although equipped with new modifications, were still essentially twenty-year-old designs.

Despite a huge national debate, the bill establishing the British Transport Commission, the organisation set up to run the nationalised railways and other forms of inland transport, was passed on 6 August 1947. For the GWR directors and 113,000 employees, from senior management to the most junior porter, who had worked so hard to recover from the Second World War, this development was difficult to accept; the company began a well-organised but ultimately unsuccessful campaign to oppose nationalisation.

Unlike the other 'Big Four' companies, the GWR was in a good financial state, and in its final year even paid a dividend of 5 per cent. Its traditions went back to 1835 and not just twenty-five years like the other 'Big Four' companies, so when the Great Western became British Railways (Western Region) on 1 January 1948 there was an air of sadness as the railway entered a new era 113 years after its birth.

London GWR

"Afloat upon ethereal tides
St. Paul's above the city rides"

This 1946 poster featuring the enduring wartime symbol of St Paul's Cathedral had more than an element of post-war patriotism in its design.

A post-war picture of a Great Western goods guard, who poses in a Swindon-built 'Toad' brake van. All GWR goods wagons were given sometimes strange code names to help identify them in telephone or telegraph communication.

GREAT WESTERN LEGACY

Following nationalisation, the Great Western had little representation within the new British Transport Commission and Railway Executive. In a final act of defiance, Sir James Milne, the last General Manager, had declined an offer to chair the Railway Executive, and Sir Allan Quartermaine, the last GWR Chief Civil Engineer, also refused the chance to be a member of the Executive. In the event, the only representative of the old company was David Blee, the former Goods Manager.

There was continuity at management level, with Keith Grand, previously assistant to Sir James Milne, becoming Chief Executive Officer of Western Region, the term 'General Manager' being seen as a relic of the old order. To those using the railway, there seemed to be minimal change initially; locomotives reappeared in Brunswick green, and carriages carried the familiar chocolate and cream livery of the pre-war GWR. Under Grand, staff battled to preserve as much Great Western tradition as possible, maintaining its pre-Grouping working practices wherever they could, and opposing the spread of standardisation, which Grand labelled as 'a fetish on British Railways'.

Even without obstruction from ex-GWR staff, there were considerable obstacles in trying to standardise its working practices in line with other regions; the most thorny issue was the instruction by the British Transport Commission that Western Region was to adopt its automatic warning system (AWS) for train safety instead of the old GWR Automatic Train Control (ATC) system, with ex-GWR men convinced that their system had a far better safety record. A related issue was the long tradition of using lower quadrant signals on the GWR. Great Western locomotives were also driven from the right-hand side of the cab, which made life very difficult for footplate staff when BR standard designs with a left-hand driving position were introduced.

The effects of nationalisation were strongly felt at Swindon, especially with the retirement of F. W. Hawksworth in 1949. The post of Chief Mechanical Engineer, like that of General Manager, was abolished and

Opposite: Swindon-built 'Warship' diesel hydraulic no. D801 *Vanguard* on a down express at Dawlish on 23 August 1961. This is still a very 'Great Western' scene, nearly fifteen years after the end of the GWR.

The nameplate of GWR 'Castle' Class no. 7007 *Great Western*. Built as *Ogmore Castle* in 1946, the engine was renamed in January 1948 in tribute to the now-abolished company, and also to the first engine built at Swindon in 1846.

departments covering Motive Power, Carriage and Wagon, and Mechanical and Electrical were created. The tight-knit staff at Swindon, where recruitment was usually from within, was changed with the appointment of newcomers, largely from the LMS. From a close-knit community, with traditions stretching back more than a century, there was great opposition to the change and a feeling that old scores were being settled. Despite these changes, Swindon habits were hard to break, and the works continued to operate in much the same way it had.

The decision to build further 'Castle' Class engines in 1946 and 1948 could be seen as complacency or defiance, or both, although the Western Region reinforced its independent outlook in the 1950s when they built a series of diesel hydraulic locomotives, instead of adopting diesel electric traction as other BR regions were doing. It was clearly no coincidence that the 'D1000' Class all carried a name beginning with the word *Western*. The 'Western', 'Warship' and 'Hymek' classes of diesel were used until the late 1970s, but were not always reliable. Whatever misgivings there might have been among Great Western traditionalists at Swindon Works, the factory nevertheless turned out considerable numbers of BR standard

Locomotive cleaners had a tough and dirty job, removing ash and clinker from locomotive smokeboxes and fireboxes. This worker at Southall is being timed by a British Railways 'time and motion' clerk.

Staff at Swindon Works prepare no. 4082 *Windsor Castle* for use on the funeral train for King George VI in February 1952.

designs, many with a clear LMS lineage. The end of an era for Swindon was the completion of 9F 2-10-0 *Evening Star*, the last steam locomotive to be built for BR and the last to be built at Swindon. Although a goods locomotive, the engine was completed at the works with much fanfare in 1960 in lined Brunswick green livery, complete with GWR-style nameplates bearing a name harking back to the days of Gooch and the broad gauge.

A 'Western' Class diesel hydraulic locomotive stands at the end of platform 1 of Paddington station. This class first entered service in 1961 and in all seventy-four were constructed, with some even built at Crewe. All were withdrawn by 1977.

The naming ceremony for British Railways 2-10-0 '9F' Class locomotive no. 92220 *Evening Star* at Swindon on 18 March 1960. The formal naming was carried out by K. W. Grand. The Mayor of Swindon can also be seen on the ceremonial platform.

However hard Grand may have tried to retain GWR traditions and practices, outside pressures had a more dramatic effect on the fortunes of the railway. Road competition grew steadily and the financial crisis gripping British Railways meant that drastic measures were inevitable. Grand's successor, J. R. Hammond, although a Western man, could do little to save the railway from the effects of the Beeching report. The wholesale closure of many GWR cross-country routes and rural branch lines changed the character of the old GWR network for good. The Western's Indian summer of nominal independence ended in 1962 with the appointment of Stanley Raymond. He had little sentiment for GWR custom and practice and made dramatic changes to the organisation, even ordering the removal of all the GWR relics and paintings that had hung on the walls of the offices at Paddington.

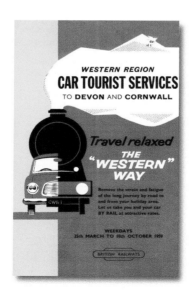

By 1959 BR management had reluctantly acknowledged that the car was here to stay, as this handbill reveals, offering motorists the chance to take their car by rail to holiday resorts.

Whilst many staff disagreed with Raymond's disregard for Great Western traditions, his actions, along with the cuts in the railway resulting from the Beeching report, ensured that a significant part of the old GWR network did survive. Under his successor, Gerald Fiennes, matters improved further; respecting old Great Western traditions, he gave a number of Class 47 diesels ex-GWR names, a practice that has continued to the present day. Subsequently, the introduction of High Speed Trains on both the West Country and Bristol–London main lines has improved travelling times significantly. Although the workforce had been much reduced since 1945, the announcement that the works at Swindon would close in 1986 was a huge shock to many in the town. It ended a proud tradition of railway engineering that stretched back more than 140 years.

With the privatisation of British Rail in the 1990s, there were hopes that a new company could be launched to honour the best customs and traditions of the old GWR. The arrangements adopted by the government provided for the separation of train operators and railway infrastructure, so that no return to the old Great Western company would be possible. Today, trains still race down Brunel's Great Western main line from London to Bristol, run by a company called 'First Great Western', but its operating practices and ethos are very different to those of the original GWR. However, it was no coincidence that the train operators' parent company chose to use 'Great Western' for at least part of their name.

Lost forever: a GWR 45xx 'Prairie' tank leaves the station at Chipping Norton in Oxfordshire. This station on the Banbury–Cheltenham route closed to passengers in 1962, and goods two years later.

The Brunel station at Charlbury in Oxfordshire is a good example of his 'chalet' style of small station and has been well restored and maintained. The effect has been improved by the addition of two GWR-style station nameboards.

Long after the GWR ceased to exist as an independent company, it is still held in great affection by many people, not all of them railway enthusiasts. This may be because much of the GWR heritage still survives. Many of the stations and structures that made the railway so famous still exist – Paddington Station, Maidenhead Bridge, parts of Swindon Works, Box Tunnel, Bristol Temple Meads and the Royal Albert Bridge at Saltash not only

The Great Western Railway Museum in Swindon pictured shortly after it opened in 1962. Its displays contained some famous GWR engines, including a replica of the broad-gauge pioneer *North Star* and the record-breaking *City of Truro*.

serve as reminders of GWR engineering prowess but are still in daily railway use, carrying trains as originally intended.

The Great Western also survives through the efforts of the railway heritage movement. The company did not always look after its own history, the best example being the scrapping of its two surviving broad-gauge locomotives, *North Star* and *Lord of the Isles*, in 1906. In the last days of steam, Swindon Borough Council and the British Transport Commission joined forces to open the Great Western Railway Museum in the town in 1962. Following the closure of the works and the redevelopment of their site, National Lottery funding finally allowed the construction of a new larger museum, 'STEAM: Museum of the GWR', in 2000.

The Didcot Railway Centre houses the Great Western Society's unique collection of GWR steam engines, coaches, wagons, buildings and small relics, and a recreation of Brunel's broad-gauge railway, based at the original 1930s Didcot locomotive shed. Many engines preserved by the society were rescued from Dai Woodham's scrapyard at Barry in South Wales. The preservation of so many ex-GWR designs there has ensured that passengers on heritage lines such as the Dean Forest, Llangollen, Severn Valley, South Devon and West Somerset railways can experience some of the atmosphere of an ex-GWR branch line behind a Swindon-built locomotive.

The Brunel era re-created: GWR mixed-gauge track work seen at the Great Western Society's Didcot Railway Centre.

PLACES TO VISIT

MUSEUMS

Didcot Railway Centre, Didcot, Oxfordshire OX11 5XP. Telephone: 01235
817200. Website: www.didcotrailwaycentre.org.uk

National Railway Museum, Leeman Road, York YO26 6XJ. Telephone: 01904
621261. Website: www.nrm.org.uk

Newton Abbot Museum and GWR Museum, St Paul's Road, Newton Abbot.
Devon. TQ4 2HP. Telephone: 01626 201121.

Pendon Museum, Long Wittenham, Didcot, Oxfordshire OX14 4QD.
Telephone 01865 407365. Website: www.pendonmuseum.com

STEAM: Museum of the Great Western Railway, Kemble Drive, Swindon,
Wiltshire SN1 2TA. Telephone: 01793 466646.
Website: www.steam-museum.org.uk

HERITAGE RAILWAYS

Birmingham Railway Museum, Tyseley Locomotive Works, Birmingham B11
2HL. Telephone: 0121 708 4965. Website: www.vintagetrains.co.uk

Bodmin &Wenford Railway, General Station, Bodmin, Cornwall PL31 1AQ.
Telephone: 01208 73555. Website:
www.bodminandwenfordrailway.co.uk

Chinnor and Princes Risborough Railway, Station Road, Chinnor, Oxfordshire,
OX39 4ER. Telephone: 01844 353535. Website:
www.chinnorrailway.co.uk

Cholsey &Wallingford Railway, Wallingford, Oxfordshire OX10 9GQ.
Telephone: 01491 835067. Website: www.cholsey-wallingford-
railway.com

Dean Forest Railway, Norchard, Lydney, Gloucestershire GL15 4ET.
Telephone: 01594 845840. Website www.deanforestrailway.co.uk

East Somerset Railway, Cranmore, Shepton Mallet, Somerset BA4 4QP.
Telephone: 01749 880417. Website: www.eastsomersetrailway.com

Gloucestershire Warwickshire Railway, Toddington, Cheltenham GL54 5DT.
Telephone: 01242 621405. Website: www.gwsr.com

Gwili Railway, Bronwydd Arms Station, Carmarthen SA33 6HT. Telephone:
01267 238213. Website: www.gwili-railway.co.uk

Llangollen Railway, Abbey Road, Llangollen, Denbighshire LL20 8SN.
Telephone: 01978 860951. Website: www.llangollen-railway.co.uk

Paignton & Dartmouth Steam Railway, Torbay Road, Paignton, Devon TQ4
6AF. Telephone: 01803 555872. Website: www.paignton-
steamrailway.co.uk

Severn Valley Railway, Bewdley, Worcestershire DY12 1BG.
Telephone: 01299 403816. Website: www.svr.co.uk

South Devon Railway, Buckfastleigh, South Devon TQ11 0DZ.
Telephone: 0845 345 1420. Website: www.southdevonrailway.org

Swindon & Cricklade Railway, Blunsdon, Swindon, Wiltshire SN25 2DA.
Telephone: 01793 771615. Website: www.swindon-cricklade-railway.org/

Vale of Rheidol Railway, Park Avenue, Aberystwyth, Ceredigion SY23 1PG.
Telephone: 01970 625819. Website: www.rheidolrailway.co.uk

Welshpool & Llanfair Railway, The Station, Llanfair Caereinion, Welshpool,
Powys SY21 0SF. Telephone: 01938 810441. Website: www.wllr.org.uk

West Somerset Railway, Minehead, Somerset TA24 5BG. Telephone: 01643
704996. Website: www.west-somerset-railway.co.uk

In addition to the above listed preserved portions of the GWR, operating examples of Great Western locomotives can be found at many other heritage railways throughout England and Wales.

FURTHER READING

Adams, Will (editor). *Encyclopedia of the Great Western Railway*. PSL, 1993.

Bryan, Tim. *All in a Day's Work: Life on the GWR*. Ian Allan, 2004.

Cattell, John, and Falconer, Keith. *Swindon: Legacy of a Railway Town*. HMSO, 1995.

Russell, Janet. *Great Western Company Servants*. Wild Swan, 1983.

Whitehouse, P., and St John Thomas, D. *The Great Western Railway: 150 Glorious Years*. David & Charles, 2002.

Vaughan, Adrian. *A Pictorial Record of Great Western Architecture*. OPC, 1977.

INDEX